River Adventures
THE YANGTZE RIVER
BY MONIKA DAVIES
BLASTOFF! DISCOVERY
BELLWETHER MEDIA • MINNEAPOLIS, MN

This edition first published in 2025 by Bellwether Media, Inc.

Library of Congress Cataloging-in-Publication Data

Names: Davies, Monika, author.
Title: The Yangtze River / by Monika Davies.
Description: Minneapolis, MN : Bellwether Media, Inc., 2025. | Series: Blastoff! Discovery : River adventures | Includes bibliographical references and index. | Audience: Ages 7-13 | Audience: Grades 4-6 | Summary: "Engaging images accompany information about the Yangtze River. The combination of high-interest subject matter and narrative text is intended for students in grades 3 through 8"– Provided by publisher.
Identifiers: LCCN 2024016626 (print) | LCCN 2024016627 (ebook) | ISBN 9798893040012 (library binding) | ISBN 9781644879337 (ebook)
Subjects: LCSH: Yangtze River (China)–Juvenile literature.
Classification: LCC DS793.Y3 D38 2025 (print) | LCC DS793.Y3 (ebook) | DDC 951.2–dc23/eng/20240513
LC record available at https://lccn.loc.gov/2024016626
LC ebook record available at https://lccn.loc.gov/2024016627

Editor: Rachael Barnes Designer: Brittany McIntosh

Printed in the United States of America, North Mankato, MN.

TABLE OF CONTENTS

THE MAGNIFICENT RIVER

CHONGQING

A group of **tourists** boards their cruise ship in Chongqing, China. The ship sails east, beginning a four-day journey on the Yangtze River. The group first stops to tour riverside temples. Later, the ship moves through three **gorges**. From the ship decks, people look up at tall green peaks. Mist blankets them. The river calmly stretches ahead.

LONG RIVER

In China, only a small part of the river is called Yangtze. Most of the river is known as *Chang Jiang*, or "long river."

The ship docks for a tour of the Three Gorges Dam. Soon, the ship sets off on the last part of the journey. The group arrives in Yichang. They look back at the Yangtze. This magnificent river is a source of energy and natural beauty.

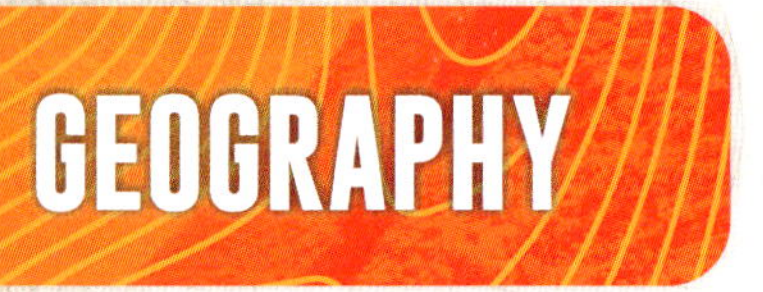

GEOGRAPHY

The Yangtze River is Asia's longest river. It is 3,915 miles (6,301 kilometers) long! Much of the river cuts through the center of China. It mostly flows east. Along its path, over 700 **tributaries** join the river.

The Yangtze begins in the Tanggula Mountains in southwestern China. The mountain range straddles Tibet and the Qinghai **province**. Melting **glacier** water races down the peaks. The water becomes the Tuotuo River. It is joined by several streams to form the Yangtze River. The upper course of the river continues, winding through the **Plateau** of Tibet. The river then drops down steep and snowy mountains.

N
W E
S
CHINA
EAST CHINA SEA
NANJING
CHONGQING
SHANGHAI
= TANGGULA MOUNTAINS

EIGHT TRIBUTARIES

Eight main tributaries add to the Yangtze River. The Yalong, Min, Jialing, and Han Rivers flow from the north to join the Yangtze. The Wu, Yuan, Xiang, and Gan Rivers travel from the south to merge with the Yangtze.

The middle course of the Yangtze runs through the hills of the Sichuan province. Flat, rich earth borders the river. Next, the river rushes past Chongqing. This city sits next to the **confluence** of the Yangtze and Jialing Rivers. The riverbanks in this region are often tall and steep.

CONFLUENCE OF THE YANGTZE AND JIALING RIVERS

HIDDEN DEPTHS

The Yangtze River has hidden depths. Parts of the river are 100 to 130 feet (30 to 40 meters) deep.

THREE GORGES REGION

The river next passes through the Three Gorges region. This area has high limestone cliffs that tower over the Yangtze. The river's middle course then reaches Yichang in the Hubei province.

WIDENING RIVER

The Yangtze River grows wider as it flows across China. In the lower course, the river is up to 2,600 feet (792 meters) wide!

YANGTZE RIVER DELTA

SHANGHAI

The Yangtze's lower course crosses a patchwork of lakes and rivers. The Yuan, Xiang, and Han Rivers join the Yangtze in this area. Several large lakes, including Dongting Lake, also drain into the Yangtze. Green rice plants dot this region.

The Yangtze next flows through the North China **Plain**. The river slows as it heads toward the Yangtze River **delta**. It passes China's largest city, Shanghai. Finally, the Yangtze empties into the East China Sea.

PLANTS AND ANIMALS

The Yangtze River **basin** is home to hundreds of **endangered** animals. Snow leopards roam across mountains and parts of the Plateau of Tibet. Giant pandas munch on bamboo in central China. Red pandas rest in nearby fir trees. Each summer, large groups of golden snub-nosed monkeys gather in cooler forests.

Finches and golden eagles fly over the Yangtze. Flat-headed Chinese giant salamanders hunt in the river. They suck their prey into their mouths!

GIANT PANDA

Life Span: 15 to 20 years
Status: vulnerable

giant panda range = ■

LEAST CONCERN	NEAR THREATENED	VULNERABLE	ENDANGERED	CRITICALLY ENDANGERED	EXTINCT IN THE WILD	EXTINCT
		▲				

Poyang Lake feeds the Yangtze and hosts a lot of wildlife. Siberian cranes fly from Russia to winter at the lake. Chinese water chestnuts rise out of the water in Poyang Lake. Yellow floating hearts cover the water's surface.

FLOATING HEARTS

CHINESE ALLIGATOR

In the river, over 350 types of fish swim and swerve through the waters. Chinese sturgeons lay their eggs in the Yangtze. Finless porpoises dip and dive in shallow parts of the river. Chinese alligators lurk at night in the Yangtze's lower course and surrounding **wetlands**. They look for snails and fish.

HUMAN HISTORY

The Yangtze is a long river with a long history. Historians believe humans may have lived in the Yangtze region as far back as 2 million years ago. Many early **settlers** chose to live near rivers. The river system made it easier to travel around the region.

CROWDED BASIN

Today, the Yangtze River basin is home to 480 million people. That means one out of every three people in China lives in the area!

Settlers herded and hunted animals on the plateau. For centuries, people also farmed the land near the river. The rich soil made it easy to grow crops for food.

YANGTZE RIVER TIMELINE

1,000 BCE
The Ba tribe live near the middle course of the Yangtze

4TH CENTURY BCE
Construction starts on the Grand Canal that connects the Yangtze with northern China

907 CE
The Ten Kingdoms period begins in the Yangtze River valley

1949
The People's Republic of China is founded and begins building dams on the Yangtze River

2020
The Chinese government passes the Yangtze River Protection Law

Starting in the 11th century BCE, the Ba tribe lived near the river's middle course. Centuries later, the Chu state came to power. They lived along the river in what is now the Hubei province.

Over time, people made changes to the river with big projects. In the 4th century BCE, work began on the Grand Canal. It grew over time. The southern part of the canal moved grain from fields near the river to cities in the north. People also built **irrigation** systems around the river. These provided water to farmland.

THE GRAND CANAL

The Grand Canal was built in sections. In 1282 CE, the Yuan Dynasty began building a new part of the canal to move grain. This section became the modern Grand Canal.

GRAND CANAL

The Ten Kingdoms period took place between 907 CE and 960 CE. Five **dynasties** ruled in the north. Ten kingdoms held land mostly south of the river. The river served as a border between the north and south.

CULTURAL CONNECTION

HANGING COFFINS

WHAT ARE THEY?

Hundreds of wooden coffins, many of which rest about 100 feet (30 meters) off the ground

WHERE ARE THEY?

In caves and on cliff faces in southern China, with many along the Yangtze River

MEANING

Higher resting places may have been believed to be closer to heaven

NANJING

In the following centuries, the Yangtze was often a battleground. Wars were fought with ships on the water. The groups in power changed over the years. Many groups placed their capital in the same area along the river. This area became modern-day Nanjing. In 1949, the People's Republic of China was founded. It began the work of building over 50,000 dams on the Yangtze.

THE RIVER TODAY

The Yangtze is still a river filled with life and endless traffic. It is considered one of the busiest rivers in the world. Huge cities have major ports along the river. Ships glide through the water, carrying goods and people.

COMING IN THIRD

The Yangtze River is the world's third-longest river! It falls behind the Amazon and Nile Rivers.

FISHING

FARMING

Around half of all food grown in China is found in the Yangtze River basin. About half of the fish eaten in China comes from the river! Over half of the rice eaten is also grown in fields the river supports.

GEZHOUBA DAM

Many deadly floods occur in China during the **monsoon** season. Water overflows throughout the Yangtze basin. The many dams along the Yangtze prevent damage from annual flooding. The dams also create **hydropower** and often make it easier to travel on the river.

The Gezhouba Dam was the first structure built to block the Yangtze. It is near Yichang. The largest dam on the Yangtze is now the Three Gorges Dam. It also is the world's largest hydropower station.

RIVER PROJECT PROFILE

THREE GORGES DAM

WHAT IS IT?

A dam near Yichang that produces the most power of any hydropower dam in the world

PURPOSE

Controls the passage of oceangoing ships and produces hydropower

COMPLETED

2006

PROTECTING THE RIVER

The Yangtze River has faced many challenges as China's economy has grown. Industries have expanded. Shipping and passenger traffic on the river have increased. Both have led to more pollution in the river and its tributaries.

Climate change also harms the river. As temperatures rise, the glaciers that feed the Yangtze are shrinking. Severe weather also causes an increase in both floods and **droughts** in the river basin. The health of the Yangtze River has a huge impact on China. Its river basin supports crops that feed much of China. Thousands of animals and plants depend on the river.

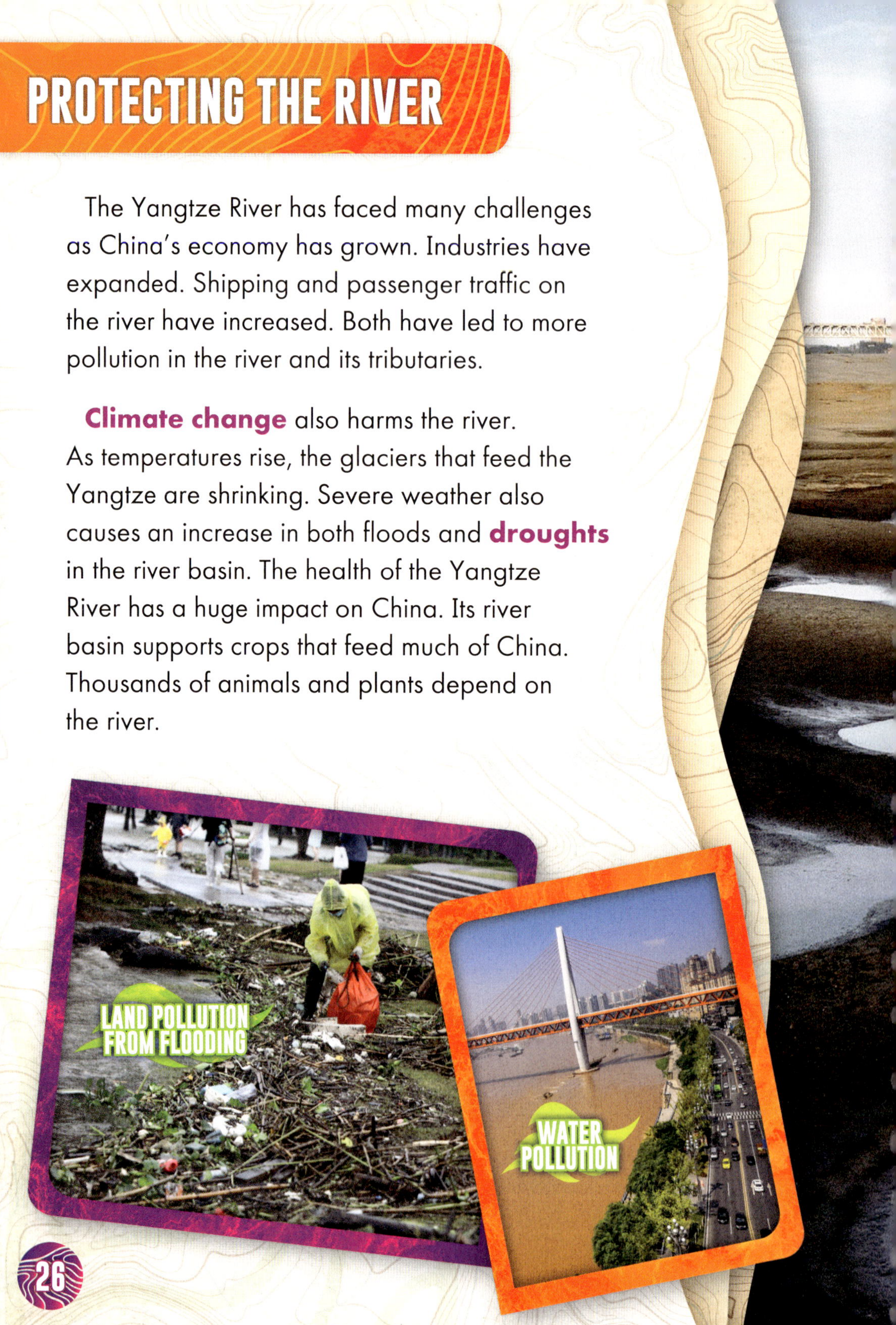

LOW WATER LEVEL
DUE TO DROUGHT

SPONGE CITIES

Parts of China are building areas called sponge cities. They are filled with grasses, willows, and other plants that take in extra water from heavy rains. Sponge cities help stop flooding in urban areas!

Decades of construction have changed the river's size and harmed the surrounding landscape. But many people are working to help the river. The Chinese government made the Yangtze River Protection Law in 2020. The law focuses on treating pollution in the water from riverside companies. It also protects the river's grasslands and wetlands.

Organizations work with farmers and fishers in the basin. They work together to keep the land, water, and wildlife healthy. With continued protection, the Yangtze River will hopefully have a long and beautiful future.

GLOSSARY

basin—the area drained by a river

climate change—a human-caused change in Earth's weather due to warming temperatures

confluence—the place where two rivers meet

delta—a land area that forms where a river flows into a large body of water

droughts—long periods of dry weather

dynasties—lines of rulers that come from the same family

endangered—at risk of disappearing forever

glacier—a massive sheet of ice that covers a large area of land

gorges—narrow canyons with steep walls

hydropower—the energy created by moving water

irrigation—related to the act or process of supplying water to an area

monsoon—related to winds that shift direction each season; monsoons bring heavy rain.

plain—a large area of flat land

plateau—an area of flat, raised land

province—an area within a country; provinces follow all the laws of the country and make some of their own laws.

settlers—people who move to live in a new region

tourists—people who travel to visit another place

tributaries—rivers and streams that flow into a larger stream, river, or lake

wetlands—areas of land that are covered with low levels of water for most of the year

TO LEARN MORE

AT THE LIBRARY

Hustad, Douglas. *Your Passport to China*. North Mankato, Minn.: Capstone Press, 2021.

Kaminski, Leah. *Ni hao, China*. Ann Arbor, Mich.: Cherry Lake Publishing, 2020.

Oachs, Emily Rose. *Ancient China*. Minneapolis, Minn.: Bellwether Media, 2020.

ON THE WEB

FACTSURFER

Factsurfer.com gives you a safe, fun way to find more information.

1. Go to www.factsurfer.com.
2. Enter "Yangtze River" into the search box and click 🔍.
3. Select your book cover to see a list of related content.

INDEX

The images in this book are reproduced through the courtesy of: Daniel Doerfler, front cover; Eric Isselee, p. 3; MyCreative, pp. 4-5; jejim, p. 5; Imaginechina Limited/ Alamy, pp. 6-7, 23 (left), 26 (left); Xinhua/ Alamy, pp. 8, 28; terimma, p. 9; Universal Images Group North America LLC/ Alamy, p. 10 (top); chuyuss, p. 10 (middle); Itemme, p. 10 (bottom); Xinhua News Agency/ Contributor/ Getty Images, p. 11 (top); CatherineScarlett, p. 11 (bottom); withGod, p. 12 (golden eagle); Dennis W Donohue, p. 12 (snow leopard); Paolo Gallo, p. 12 (red panda); Wang LiQiang, p. 12 (golden snub-nosed monkey); tristan tan, p. 12 (Chinese giant salamander); AKKHARAT JARUSILAWONG, p. 13; Rudmer Zwerver, p. 14 (top); Danny Ye, p. 14 (bottom); EarnestTse, p. 15; Keren Su/China Span/ Alamy, p. 16; Bildagentur-online/ Contributor/ Getty Images, pp. 16-17; jejim120/ Alamy, p. 18 (top); Julia Hiebaum/ Alamy, p. 18 (middle); Cynthia Lee/ Alamy, p. 18 (bottom); Rick Wang, p. 19 (top); mauritius images GmbH/ Alamy, p. 19 (bottom); Robert Burch/ Alamy, p. 20; Joshua Davenport, p. 21; Yong nian Gui/ Alamy, pp. 22-23; Claudine Klodien/ Alamy, p. 23 (right); Imago/ Alamy, p. 24; powerofforever, p. 25; khlongwangchao, p. 26 (right); Sipa USA/ Alamy, pp. 26-27; Jakrit Jiraratwaro, pp. 28-29; sathit savettanant, p. 31.